W9-DCU-894
FEB 11 2020

WHAT'S ACTIVISM?

By Leslie Beckett

Published in 2020 by
KidHaven Publishing, an Imprint of Greenhaven Publishing, LLC
353 3rd Avenue
Suite 255
New York, NY 10010

Designer: Andrea Davison-Bartolotta
Editor: Katie Kawa

Photo credits: Cover (top) Rawpixel.com/Shutterstock.com; cover (bottom) Dmytro Zinkevych/Shutterstock.com; pp. 4, 7 (top), 9 (main) Rena Schild/Shutterstock.com; p. 5 Joseph Sohm/Shutterstock.com; p. 6 Michael Ochs Archives/Getty Images; p. 7 (bottom) Central Press/Getty Images; p. 9 (inset) Karl_Sonnenberg/Shutterstock.com; pp. 9 (background), 11 (background) Attitude/Shutterstock.com; p. 11 (main) Noam Galai/WireImage/Getty Images; p. 11 (inset) JStone/Shutterstock.com; p. 12 betto rodrigues/Shutterstock.com; p. 13 Albisoima/Shutterstock.com; p. 15 Ken Wolter/Shutterstock.com; p. 17 (top left) Alfa Photostudio/Shutterstock.com; p. 17 (top right) Africa Studio/Shutterstock.com; p. 17 (bottom right) © iStockphoto.com/Image Source; p. 17 (bottom left) Monkey Business Images/Shutterstock.com; p. 19 fizkes/Shutterstock.com; p. 20 Ryan Rodrick Beiler/Shutterstock.com; p. 21 Olga Starikova/Shutterstock.com.

Library of Congress Cataloging-in-Publication Data

Names: Beckett, Leslie, author.
Title: What's activism? / Leslie Beckett.
Description: New York : KidHaven Publishing, [2020] | Series: What's the
  issue? | Includes index.
Identifiers: LCCN 2019005209 (print) | LCCN 2019007972 (ebook) | ISBN
  9781534567429 (eBook) | ISBN 9781534567405 (pbk. book) | ISBN
  9781534567412 (library bound book) | ISBN 9781534531284 (6 pack)
Subjects: LCSH: Children–Political activity–Juvenile literature. |
  Political participation–Juvenile literature. | Social action–Juvenile
  literature.
Classification: LCC HQ784.P5 (ebook) | LCC HQ784.P5 B43 2020 (print) | DDC
  320.083–dc23
LC record available at https://lccn.loc.gov/2019005209

Printed in the United States of America

CPSIA compliance information: Batch #BS19KL: For further information contact Greenhaven Publishing LLC, New York, New York at 1-844-317-7404.

Please visit our website, www.greenhavenpublishing.com. For a free color catalog of all our high-quality books, call toll free 1-844-317-7404 or fax 1-844-317-7405.

CONTENTS

Turning Feelings into Action

Everyone has causes they care about. Some people feel strongly about animal rights. Others care about making sure all people are treated fairly. Maybe you care about **protecting** the **environment**.

When people feel strongly about issues in the world around them, they often want to turn those feelings into action. This is called activism. Activists work hard to make the world a better place. Activism isn't just for adults—kids can also do their part to fight for causes that matter to them!

Facing the Facts 🔍

More than half of Americans between the ages of 13 and 21 believe the actions of ordinary citizens can **affect** decisions made by the government about important issues.

Activists fight for change and stand up for what they believe, and they do this in many different ways. Anyone can be an activist!

A Powerful Example

Activism isn't easy! Activists work hard, and they sometimes put themselves in danger to stand up for what they believe. Some activists have even ended up in jail for fighting against laws they feel are unfair.

During the civil rights movement in the 1950s and 1960s, activists fought against unfair laws that kept African Americans from having equal rights. These activists, including Dr. Martin Luther King Jr., were sometimes put in jail or hurt by people who didn't believe in equality. However, they kept fighting for what they believed was right.

Facing the Facts

Activism in the 1960s included more than just the civil rights movement. Activists at that time were also **involved** in the fight for women's rights and spoke out strongly against war.

6

Activism isn't new. People have been fighting to make the world a better place throughout history. Today's activists can learn a lot from those who came before them.

A New Age of Activism

Activists have been hard at work throughout history, and they're continuing to work to build a better world today. In fact, many people believe we're living in a new age of activism, in which more people than ever are joining together to fight for causes they care about.

Starting in 2017, many marches have been held in Washington, D.C., and throughout the rest of the United States to call attention to important issues. Activists have **organized** marches for women's rights, against gun **violence**, and in support of science and many other causes. Millions of people have taken part in these marches!

Facing the Facts

Many activists today fight for the rights of immigrants—people who come to another country to live there. For example, a group called United We Dream is run by young immigrant activists who are working to make sure all immigrants are treated fairly.

Activists know it's better to join together than to work alone. When people work together, they can change the world!

Students Lead the Way

Adults are often the faces of activism, but young people have also played an important part in activist movements in the past and present. Students often led **protests** during the civil rights movement, and students are still voices for change in their communities today.

For example, a group of high school students became activists after a deadly shooting at their school in Parkland, Florida, in 2018. They began to speak out in favor of stronger gun control laws. They even planned the March for Our Lives in Washington, D.C., where adults and young people joined together to take a stand against gun violence.

The students who led the March for Our Lives have continued their activism by leading drives to get young people to register, or sign up, to vote. Americans can't vote until they turn 18, but they can find other ways to fight for change until they reach that age.

Facing the Facts

One of the most famous young activists is Malala Yousafzai. When she lived in Pakistan, she fought for the right for all girls to go to school, but she was shot by someone who wanted her to stop speaking out. She didn't let that stop her, though, and she's become one of the most important figures in the fight for girls' education around the world.

11

The First Step

With so many causes to care about, it can be hard to decide where to start on the path to becoming an activist. The best way to begin is by learning as much as you can about what's happening in the world. Talking to a trusted adult is a good way to learn more—and to get them involved in activism too!

When you find an issue you care about, learn about the ways you can turn that caring into action. For example, you can write a letter to a government leader in your community about the issue.

Facing the Facts 🔍

As of January 2019, some of the issues Americans cared about most were the way the government was being run, immigration, health care, and making sure all people were treated with respect.

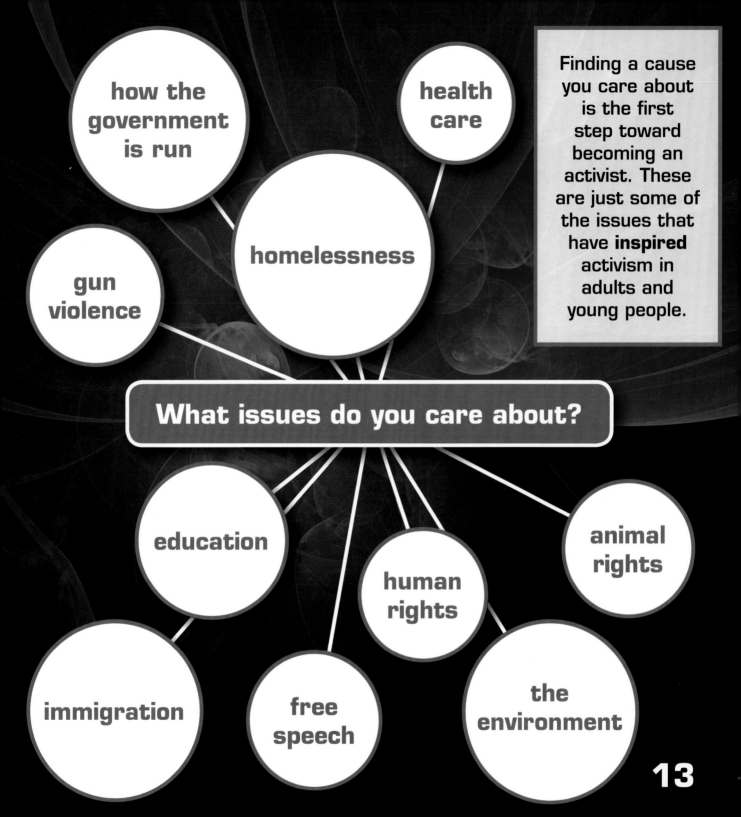

how the government is run

health care

homelessness

gun violence

Finding a cause you care about is the first step toward becoming an activist. These are just some of the issues that have **inspired** activism in adults and young people.

What issues do you care about?

education

animal rights

human rights

immigration

free speech

the environment

13

Marching for Change

When many people think of activism, they think of marches. At these events, you can meet other activists and speak out about issues that matter to you. Marches often draw big crowds and a lot of attention. Activists use that attention to educate people about important issues and to let leaders know changes need to be made.

It's important to be safe and to follow the rules at a march. If you want to go to a march, ask a trusted adult to take you. You can take friends with you too!

Facing the Facts

The First **Amendment** to the U.S. Constitution—the document that set up how the country is run—gives Americans freedom of speech, freedom to gather in groups, and freedom to ask the government to fix things that are wrong. These freedoms are all exercised when activists gather together to march.

Marches often make the local and national news, and this helps activists get their message to a large number of people, including government leaders.

15

Other Ways to Get Involved

Writing letters and marching aren't the only ways to get involved in activism. You can raise money for a cause you care about, such as helping immigrants. You can also organize a day to clean up a local park if environmental activism means a lot to you.

Activism can happen in your school community too. If you want to change something at your school, you can write about it in your school newspaper or run for student government. You can even create a club or group at school that deals with issues such as animal rights or respect for all people.

Facing the Facts

Artists can be activists too! "Artivism" is activism through art, such as painting, dance, or movies. These works of art show problems in the world and inspire people to fix those problems.

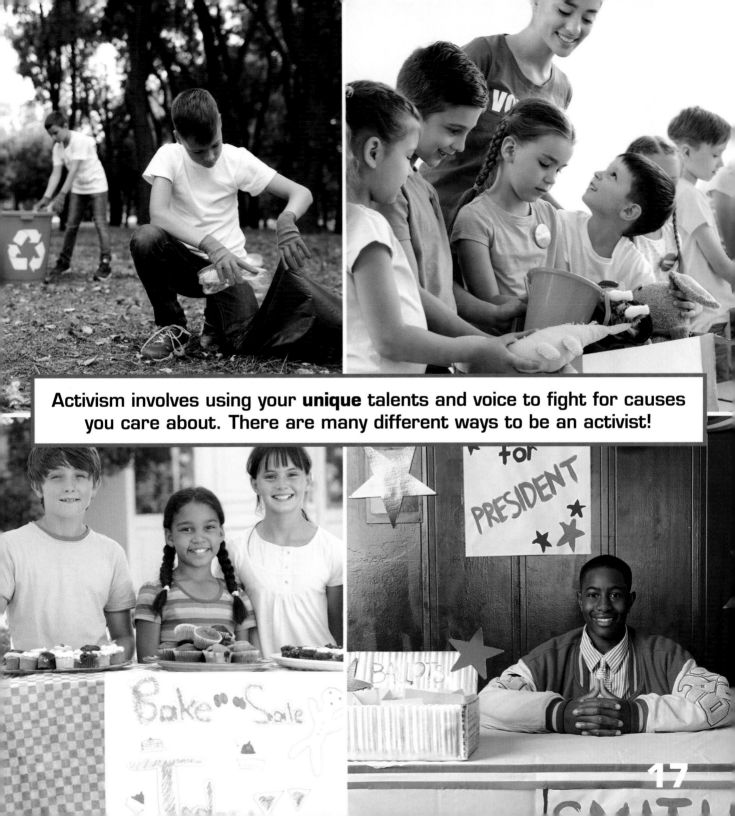

Activism involves using your **unique** talents and voice to fight for causes you care about. There are many different ways to be an activist!

Online Activism

Some people use **social media platforms** to get involved with activism. They share news stories and spread messages about issues that matter to them. People who do this believe they're educating others and calling attention to problems in the world.

However, other people believe this isn't really activism. They believe people who post about issues online without doing anything about them in person aren't taking enough action to really change things. Many people think activism can begin online but needs to happen in the world beyond our screens too.

Facing the Facts

Hacktivism happens when people get illegal **access** to computer systems to shut them down or share secret **information** as a way to call attention to a cause or create change. Some people believe hacktivists are breaking the law for a good reason, while others believe their actions do more harm than good.

Social media can be a helpful tool for activists. It can be used to get leaders' attention or to educate people about issues. However, it can also lead people to believe they're doing enough to help others when there's much more to be done.

You Can Make a Difference!

When people work hard to fight for fairness, to protect the environment, and to call attention to other important causes, they can change the world! Activists don't let problems make them feel helpless or hopeless. They believe they can make a difference, and they turn that belief into action.

No act of activism is too small. Every letter to a government leader, every dollar raised for an important cause, and every person who comes to a march matters. How can you get involved in activism in your community?

Facing the Facts 🔍

A 2018 study showed that young people who were involved in activism got farther in school and got better jobs than young people who weren't active citizens.

WHAT CAN YOU DO?

Learn about important issues in your community and around the world, and think about which ones matter most to you.

Ask a trusted adult to take you to a march for a cause you care about.

Write letters to government leaders about issues that matter to you.

Raise money for activist groups.

Ask school officials if you can create an activist club or group at your school.

Talk to your friends about ways you can make a difference in the world around you.

Talk to a trusted adult about problems in the world and what can be done to fix them.

These are some of the ways you can get started as an activist. Remember to choose activities that make you feel comfortable and safe. If you don't want to go to a march, you can find many other ways to get involved in activism!

GLOSSARY

access: The ability to use or have something.

affect: To produce an effect on something.

amendment: A change in the words or meaning of a law or document, such as a constitution.

environment: The natural world around us.

information: Knowledge or facts about something.

inspire: To move someone to do something great.

involve: To take part in.

organize: To set up and plan an event.

protect: To keep safe.

protest: An event in which people gather to show they do not like something.

social media platforms: Websites and applications, or apps, that allow users to interact with each other and create online communities.

unique: Special or different from anything else.

violence: The use of force to harm someone.

FOR MORE INFORMATION

WEBSITES

Civil Rights Movement Timeline

www.history.com/topics/civil-rights-movement/civil-rights-movement-timeline

The civil rights movement is one of the most powerful examples of activism in U.S. history, and this timeline highlights some of the movement's most important events.

Malala's Story

www.malala.org/malalas-story

Malala Yousafzai is one of the most important young activists in the world today, and her story proves that no one is too young to fight for what they believe is right.

BOOKS

Keppeler, Jill. *Be an Activist!* New York, NY: Gareth Stevens Publishing, 2019.

Mortmain, Beatrice. *Social Activism: Working Together to Create Change in Our Society.* New York, NY: PowerKids Press, 2018.

Wood, John. *Activism & Volunteering.* New York, NY: Crabtree Publishing, 2018.

INDEX